*L*atin *A*merican *H*oldings in the University of New Mexico Library

ATONATIUH, ó SOL DE AGUA

An
Illustrated
History
and Guide

Written & Compiled by Russ Davidson

UNM University Libraries / *Western Edge Press*

ACKNOWLEDGEMENTS

This publication was funded in part by contributions from the University Libraries' Aida Alves Gerdes and Thomas Bell Endowments. The assistance provided by Library and University staff in locating and using photographs and illustrations and furthering research into the history and content of particular collections is gratefully acknowledged.

PART TITLE: Drawing of an armadillo, from Edward R. Alston, *Mammalia* (London: R.H. Porter, 1879-1882), plate 20 [Biologia centrali-americana series].

FRONTISPIECE: Exterior view of west façade of Zimmerman Library, by Tyler Dingee, circa 1945. [UNM: Buildings: Library, Zimmerman 1936-1965. Box 988-009-018, folder 988-013-0010.] Pictorial Collections, Center for Southwest Research/Special Collections, UNM University Libraries.

TITLE PAGE: representation of Atonatiuh [Water Sun], a central element in Aztec cosmology, from *El Centenario* (Oaxaca) 1, no. 4 (15 Nov. 1910), facing p. 90.

ISBN: 1-889921-18-1

Printed in China

Photography by Addison Doty, Santa Fe, New Mexico

Designed and produced by Jim Mafchir, Western Edge Press

CONTENTS

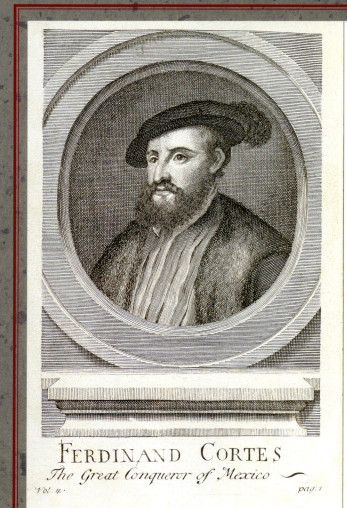

FERDINAND CORTES
The Great Conqueror of Mexico

Vol. 4.

pag. 1

THE GENERAL
HISTORY
OF THE VAST
CONTINENT *and* ISLANDS
O F
AMERICA,
Commonly call'd, THE
WEST-INDIES,
F R O M
The FIRST DISCOVERY thereof:
With the Beſt Accounts the People could give of their
ANTIQUITIES.
Collected from the Original RELATIONS
ſent to the Kings of *SPAIN*.

By *ANTONIO DE HERRERA*,
Hiſtoriographer to His CATHOLICK MAJESTY.

Tranſlated into *Engliſh* by Capt. JOHN STEVENS.

VOL. IV.

Illuſtrated with CUTTS *and* MAPS.

LONDON:
Printed for JER. BATLEY at the *Dove* in *Pater-noſter-row.*
M.DCC.XXVI.

Frontispiece and title page, from Vol. 1, *The General History of the Vast Continent and Islands of America…* 6 vols. (London: Printed for J. Batley, 1725-26), an abridged and notoriously inaccurate translation of Antonio de Herrera y Tordesillas' work, *Historia general de los hechos de los castellanos en las islas y tierra firme del mar océano*, first published in Madrid in 1601.

Lithograph by Santiago Hernández, from Gustavo Baz, *Historia del ferrocarril mexicano. . .* (Mexico: Gallo y Cía., 1874), facing p. 248.

1

*B*ACKGROUND & EARLY HISTORY

—— UNM's enduring interest in Latin America reaches back to the early years of the previous century, when the term "Pan-Americanism" was used to describe one of the University's main objectives. The ensuing decades have seen this commitment reaffirmed on many occasions, a recent example being President Richard Peck's (1990-1998) designation of UNM as a "University for the Americas." No figure, however, deserves more credit for establishing and building UNM's reputation in Latin American and Hispanic studies than its seventh president, James F. Zimmerman (1927-1944). For Zimmerman, the Latin American connection was organic to New Mexico, a natural extension of its history and traditions. Indeed, a fact sometimes overlooked by recent immigrants to the state is that by the time of Zimmerman's presidency, New Mexico had spent twice as many years as part of the Spanish Empire than it had as part of the United States. Furthermore, some fifty percent of its population continued to have Spanish as their native language. Zimmerman also understood that while the University might capitalize on this history to build a major academic program in Latin American studies, its success would only be temporary unless it also developed library holdings of comparable strength and distinction. As he wrote in the University's 1939-41 *Biennial Report* to the state legislature: "The supreme opportunity of the University for outstanding regional and national service lies in the various fields of Latin American activities. The bonds which exist between us and our neighbors to the South are not only geographic, but linguistic and cultural . . . The greatest single drawback to the advancement of our work in the Latin American field is our lack of books." When Zimmerman wrote these words, UNM had already made significant strides toward realizing his vision. It had recruited one of the most distinguished Latin Americanist faculties in the United States, inaugurated its pioneering School of Inter-American Affairs, and secured the first of many grants from foundations and government agencies

Photograph of James F. Zimmerman, circa 1935. University Archives, Center for Southwest Research/Special Collections, UNM University Libraries.

Bookplate of the Catron Collection.

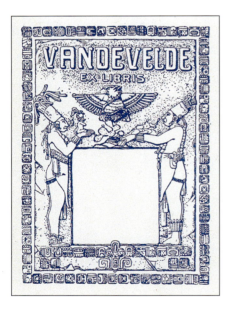

Bookplate of Paul Van de Velde.

in support of the larger effort. With Zimmerman's active involvement, it had also taken the initial steps toward addressing the "lack of books."

THE CORNERSTONES ARE LAID: ACQUISITION OF THE CATRON AND VAN DE VELDE LIBRARIES

In the development of the Library's Latin American holdings, the year 1939 proved decisive. In that year, two private libraries of exceptional merit were acquired by the University. The first had been collected by the Catron family of New Mexico (and principally by its patriarch—lawyer, banker, and political figure, Thomas B. Catron); the second by Paul Van de Velde, a Belgian mining engineer who had resided in Mexico for nineteen years. Both libraries contained nearly 10,000 volumes, including many thousands of rare and scarce imprints from Mexico and Spain. Catron's library (portions of which were received by UNM before and after 1939) had an interesting provenance. A significant part of it had been the personal library of Padre Agustín Fischer, who had served as confessor and private secretary to Emperor Maximilian. Catron had acquired the library in 1890, when he sent Adolf Bandelier—a friend of his and of Fischer's—to Mexico to purchase it. The library, rich in imprints from the 17th and 18th centuries (with many 16th-century imprints as well) focusing on the history of religious life and institutions in Spain and colonial Mexico, had been stored in the Augustinian Monastery in Guadalajara since Fischer's death in 1887. Catron's library also included many 19th-century Mexican publications and government documents, as well as numerous volumes dealing with broader Latin American themes and topics. Its value to UNM, and to scholars generally, was summed up by the eminent historian and archivist, George P. Hammond (then serving as Chairman of the University's History Department and as Dean of its Graduate School): ". . . one of the most significant collections in the Southwest for the study of Latin American history, economics, anthropology, government, sociology, and other subjects. It is not too much to say that the richness of this collection has never been duplicated in the region." This characterization holds equally true today, since many of the early Spanish and Mexican imprints in Catron's library remain the only copies to be found in the region.

Regarding the Van de Velde library, Hammond made far stronger claims. Describing its significance after its purchase in 1939, he wrote: "The value to the University of the collection can scarcely be overlooked. It lays the basis for a library as important...as the Bancroft Library is to the University of California or the García Collection to the University of Texas." These were challenging comparisons, but Hammond knew them to be valid, for as a source of specialized Mexicana, Paul Van de Velde's library possessed a wide range of unique materials. Preeminent among them were rare Indian

grammars and dictionaries, in both manuscript and printed form, produced between the 16th and 19th centuries as well as other scarce imprints on the languages and ethnohistory of southern Mexico, extensive source material in all formats on the political, cultural, and natural history of 19th-century Mexico, and a body of Oaxacan research materials of unrivaled scope and depth. While perhaps a third to half of the Catron library was a vintage 19th-century "Gentleman's Library," containing handsome sets of European and American history and literature, Van de Velde's library—though numbering a great many rare and uncommon works—was a working collection, assembled for scholarly and research purposes by a man steeped in Mesoamerican history and bibliography. Virtually all of its nearly 10,000 volumes had been published in Mexico. Thus it was that the sage bookman Henry Raup Wagner, when asked by Hammond how much Van de Velde's library was worth (for Wagner had personally inspected it), replied succinctly, "George, such a collection is worth whatever you have to pay for it." Van de Velde's library, too, had a colorful provenance. Many of its publications on the languages, archaeology, and history of Mexico in the Pre-Columbian and colonial periods had formed part of the library of the Mexican scholar and public official, Antonio Peñafiel. Van de Velde acquired them, along with some of Peñafiel's personal papers and unpublished manuscripts, from the latter's estate. Van de Velde's library also contained a major collection on the French Intervention (1862-1867) in Mexico, which he had purchased from Benjamín Barrios, whose mother had served as a Lady-in-Waiting to Empress Carlotta.

Thus, on the strength of these two acquisitions occurring within a single year, the UNM Library not only substantially erased its

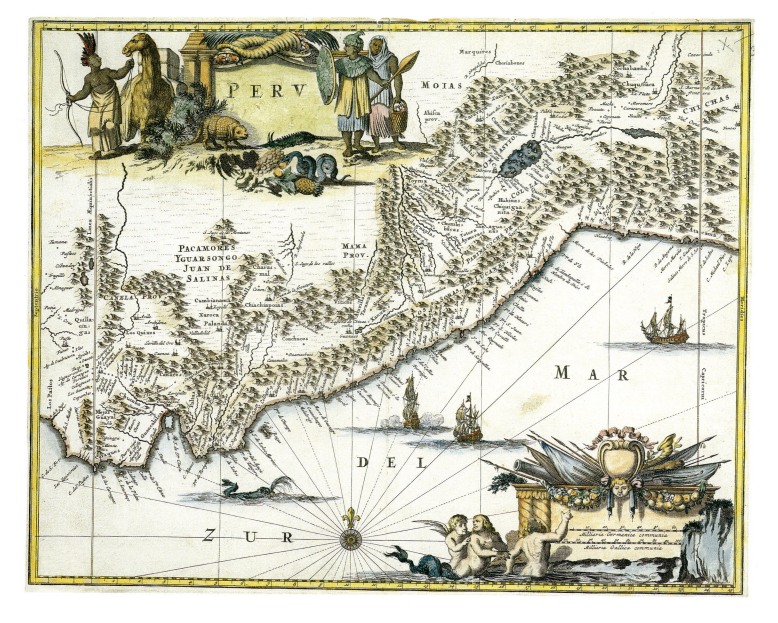

Map of Peru, likely dating from the early 1700s. Map & Geographic Information Center, Centennial Science and Engineering Library, University of New Mexico.

"lack of books" in the Latin American field but also created the nucleus of an expanding rare book collection. The growth and shaping of the Library's Latin American holdings were complemented during these early years by two related developments; a multi-year project to assemble a comprehensive collection of archival materials that would document the history of New Mexico under Spanish rule, and a concerted effort—again led by President Zimmerman—to obtain foundation and government support to further enlarge and enrich the Library's Latin American collection.

THE NEW MEXICO ARCHIVES COLLECTION & THE ATTRACTION OF OUTSIDE FUNDING

President Zimmerman's theory of the New World was a little like historian Herbert Bolton's; the Americas, in his view, shared a com-

EDIFICIO MEXICANO.
(De fotografia directa;)

LIT. H: IRIARTE, MÉXICO.

mon history. And within this trajectory, New Mexico occupied a special place; here, three major cultural traditions of the region—Indian, Hispanic, and Anglo—intersected and converged with a particular richness and intensity. This heritage had endowed the state with a singular opportunity, or as Joaquín Ortega—first Director of UNM's School of Inter-American Affairs and, later, editor of the *New Mexico Quarterly*, expressed it— ". . . there is no place in this hemisphere better equipped than New Mexico to become a synthesis of the Americas." Guided by Zimmerman's vision, the University had in part defined its mission around this principle. It thus drew to its faculty a group of scholars who were committed to studying New Mexico, and to exploring its history, as part of the broader Hispanic world, a world shaped and still heavily influenced by the Native American and Spanish presence. Encouraged and assisted by Hammond, two members of the UNM History Department, Lansing Bloom and France V. Scholes, traveled to archives in Spain, Mexico, the Vatican, and elsewhere to photocopy and microfilm documents pertaining to the history of New Mexico (and other areas of the Viceroyalty of New Spain) from the beginnings of Spanish conquest and colonization to 1840. Although they focused primarily on the *Archivo de Indias*, in Seville,

Illustration of the Mexican Pavilion, constructed for the Paris Exposition of 1889, in José F. Godoy, *México en París . . .* (Mexico: Tip. de Alfonso E. López, 1888 & Tip. José F. Godoy, 1890), facing p. 224.

Left: Oil painting of Joaquín Ortega. [Date and artist unknown.] Department of Spanish & Portuguese, Ortega Hall, University of New Mexico.

Right: Photograph of France V. Scholes, early 1970s (?). [Unprocessed Scholes Collection, Folder 1.] Pictorial Collections, Center for Southwest Research/Special Collections, UNM University Libraries.

and the *Archivo General de la Nación*, in Mexico City; the three historians also found key source material in the *Archivo Histórico Nacional*, *Biblioteca Nacional*, *Real Academia de la Historia*, *Archivo de Protocolos*, and *Archivo de Simancas* in Spain; the *Museo Nacional*, *Biblioteca Nacional*, and *Archivo Histórico Militar* in Mexico City, and the Laurentian Library, in Florence. The result of their effort, which lasted more than a decade, was the founding of the Library's "*New Mexico Archives Collection*," comprising many thousands of documents contained, initially, in some 675 bound volumes. Now called the *AGI* and *AGN* Collection, this archive continues to draw scholars from throughout Latin America, Europe, and the United States. The Project had attracted the support of the Historical Records Survey, an arm of the Works Progress Administration, and also received support from two historical commissions: the Coronado Cuarto Centennial Commission, formed in 1935 by the state legislature (and chaired by President Zimmerman) to commemorate the 400th anniversary of Francisco Vásquez de Coronado's 1540 *entrada*, and the Bandelier Centennial Commission, organized in 1937 to commemorate the 100th anniversary of Adolph Bandelier's birth in 1840. The Bandelier celebration fueled a notable archival discovery, for in 1938, while consulting the Vatican Archives, Bloom encountered and had photographed the four volumes of colored illustrations (and accompanying atlas) that Bandelier had made of the Franciscan Missions of New Mexico. These landmark sketches had been missing since Adolph Bandelier first sent them to the

Vatican from Santa Fe in 1888.

The formation of the *New Mexico Archives Collection*, to which France Scholes continued to add in later years, was instrumental in making the University of New Mexico a leading center for research into Spanish colonial history. In subsequent years, the Library widened and deepened this strength by acquiring additional groups of primary source material, from Spanish, Mexican and Latin American archives, documenting aspects of daily life and imperial administration across Spain's New World empire.

These and other initiatives of the 1930s and 1940s had given UNM a national reputation in the field of Latin American studies and laid the foundation for an equally prominent library collection. Nevertheless, while New Mexico may have been rich in tradition, it was poor in revenue. Sustained progress toward achieving the University's goals would depend, as President Zimmerman clearly saw, upon securing resources and financial support from sources outside the state. Long before the term "networking" had entered the lexicon, he employed its techniques (as did many of the Latin Americanist faculty) to compete successfully for foundation and government grants and to elicit significant donations of scholarly materials. In the early 1940s, for example, the Rockefeller Foundation awarded the Library a multi-year grant of $25,000 to help it expand its Latin American holdings. Large donations of Latin American materials were periodically made to the UNM Library, in the 1930s and 1940s, by the Carnegie Corporation, the Library of Congress,

Jesús Guerrero Galván, *Unity of the Americas*. Fresco painted by Guerrero during his time as artist-in-residence at the University of New Mexico, 1942-43. Main Floor of Scholes Hall, University of New Mexico.

Title page, from *Istoria o breuissima relatione . . .* (Venice: Presso M. Ginammi, 1630), an early Italian translation of Bartolomé de Las Casas' tract, *Brevísima relación . . .*, accompanied by an image of Las Casas, from *Historia de las Indias*, 2 vols. (Mexico: Imp. y Lit. I. Paz, 1877), frontispiece to Vol. 1.

and the war-time Office of the Coordinator of Inter-American Affairs. Funds from the latter agency, and from the State Department and the Department of Agriculture, were also awarded to the University to strengthen its library holdings on Latin America. Individuals likewise proved a fruitful source of donations during these early years. In 1945, Hammond himself gave 606 specialized Latin American monographs to the Library. Scholes was a frequent donor, as was the New Mexico writer and Latin American traveler, Erna Fergusson.

Although such gifts and grants strengthened the Library's Latin American holdings, they were still highly limited in many areas, consistently outpaced by the University's rapidly growing program in Latin American studies and Inter-American relations. The outbreak of war in Europe had brought increased concern for hemispheric security and raised the profile of Latin America in the United States. President Zimmerman leveraged this development to enlarge the University's interest and activities in the region. Even in 1939, UNM's academic program in Latin American studies stood out in comparison to similar programs in much larger universities. A survey carried out in that year found that UNM offered 37 courses, spread among 10 departments, with specific Latin American content. Furthermore, the curriculum displayed an impressive degree of specialization, incorporating such courses as "Ethnobiology of the New World," "Rural Sociology of Latin America," and "Mexican and New Mexican Folk Dance." A second survey conducted only two years later indicated that the number of courses concentrating on Latin America had grown to 47. President Zimmerman's steadfast efforts to build up the program had clearly succeeded. The founding of the University's School of Inter-American Affairs (SIAA) in 1941 crystallized this success, while also bringing new challenges to the Library. A broader range of courses and the adoption of a graduate program in Latin American studies necessarily required that the Library expand its collecting efforts on Latin America. To some extent, this need was fulfilled through the succession of grants that Zimmerman, Ortega, and others obtained during the 1940s. The faculty associated with the SIAA also actively promoted the exchange of publications between UNM and universities in Latin America and, whenever possible, incorporated the acquisition of research materials into the School's funding proposals. Their desire to develop the Latin American collection and to enhance its stature and services was evident in a proposal formulated in the early 1940s to construct a new Latin American Library. Although there was considerable logic behind the plan, it did not go forward owing to the lack of resources.

Buenos Ayrean Countryman.

Published by Smith, Elder & Cº London 1852.

"Buenos Aires Countryman," from William MacCann, *Two Thousand Miles' Ride through the Argentine Provinces* . . . 2 vols. (London: Smith, Elder & Co., et al.,1853), frontispiece to Vol. 2.

"*Button Sound, Tierra del Fuego,*" from William Parker Snow, *A Two Years' Cruise off Tierra del Fuego . . .* 2 vols. in 1 (London: Longman, et al., 1857), facing p. 54.

2

LATER DECADES

—— President Zimmerman's death in 1944, followed by George Hammond's departure from the University in 1946 and Joaquín Ortega's retirement in 1951, deprived UNM's program in Latin American studies of three of its most committed advocates. Nonetheless, their focus on Latin America had taken firm root in the institution, so that the momentum generated by their work carried forward. During the 1950s and 1960s, expenditures by the Library for Latin American materials were supplemented by major grants awarded by the Ford Foundation and the federal government, under the National Defense Education Act. Supported by these grants and other special funding, the Library began systematically to expand the scope of its Latin American holdings. The earlier concentration on Mexico was now broadened to encompass all of Latin America, with a particular emphasis placed on Brazil. As an indication of the growing strength of this segment of the collection, a catalogue of the Library's Luso-Brazilian materials (published by Scarecrow Press in 1970), listed more than 10,000 titles held as of mid-1968. Were a similar catalogue produced today for the UNM University Libraries, its total number of titles would exceed this figure four or five-fold. Much of the credit for building up the Luso-Brazilian holdings in this period is given to the Portuguese languages and literature professor, Albert Lopes.

Although the two and a half decades that followed President Zimmerman's death were years of steady expansion of the Latin American collection, the 1970s marked the advent of a new and more vigorous stage in the development of Latin American holdings at UNM. The three decades that began in the early 1970s have been characterized by extraordinary growth and by the adoption of new approaches to acquiring and accessing materials and to providing services to students, scholars, and the public. The profile and content of the collection have changed in parallel fashion, encompassing new subject and topical fields as well as new types of material and new formats. From an early emphasis on history, anthropology, and Spanish language and literature, the collection has grown to include all fields of study in the social sciences, humanities, and fine arts. Material is also acquired in selected scientific fields, in fields of professional study, such as public administration and public health, and to support dual Master's degree programs in Latin American studies and business administration/international management, community and regional planning, law, nursing, and education. During the 1960s and 1970s, a greater emphasis began to be placed on acquiring reference materials—encyclopedias, dictionaries, bibliographies, indexes, and the printed catalogs of other library collections—along with government publications, as well as documents and reports issued by regional and inter-hemispheric agencies. The periodical collection was also expanded, as subscriptions were entered for an increasing number of journals, magazines, newspapers, and newsletters. In addition, serial backfiles and large archival and research sets were acquired in microform and subsequently on compact disk. Today, the UNM Latin American collection contains, in round numbers, 450,000 books, pamphlets, and bound periodicals, 11,000 posters and broadsheets, 5,000 photographs, 350 linear feet of manuscripts, 8,000 maps, more than half a million microform units, and numerous other items in the form of videos, sound recordings, films, CD's, and memorabilia.

Recent advances in information technology and the blooming of the Internet and World Wide Web have radically altered the library landscape, opening new avenues of scholarly communication and creating new opportunities and methods for producing and disseminating research material. The UNM Library has taken full advantage of these developments, and its community of Latin Americanists—students, faculty, University staff, and visiting scholars—have access to a diverse, ever-expanding range of material in electronic format.

Some of the most noteworthy changes affecting the Latin American collection in recent years have occurred in the area of special collections. Building on the Catron and Van de Velde acquisitions, the Library has added extensively to its holdings of rare and scarce Mexicana and developed new strengths in Latin American visual resources, with a particular emphasis on photography, fine press and artists' books, and popular graphic material. These and other unique resources, outlined below, offer Latin American scholars significant opportunities for original research.

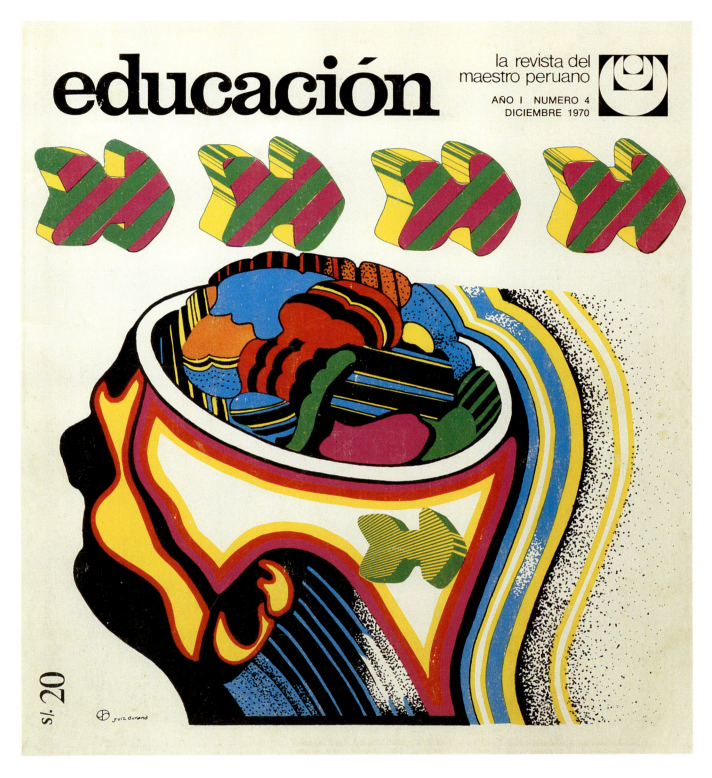

Pop art-influenced cover of the Peruvian education journal, *Educación* 1, No. 4 (December 1970). Cover design by Jesús Ruiz Durand.

Mauricio Yáñez, Mexico. *Mariachi Coculense*. Photo postcard from the 1920s. [Mexico: Selected Photographers, Folder Yáñez: 2000-001-0013.] Pictorial Collections, Center for Southwest Research/Special Collections, UNM University Libraries.

3

PROFILE OF LATIN AMERICAN COLLECTIONS

LITERATURE AND THE ARTS

Music

Two related collections, the *John Donald Robb Archive of Southwestern Music* and the *John Donald Robb Papers*, constitute a major source for the study of Latin American folk music. Created in 1964, the Archive houses nearly 40 individual collections and contains more than 1,600 reels of audio tape. The Latin American components include field recordings from Mexico, El Salvador, Venezuela, Chile, Argentina, and Jamaica as well as oral histories, interviews, and transcriptions of songs and dances documenting the Indian and Hispanic musical traditions of Mexico. It is rich in songs of the Mexican Revolution and offers many examples of *rancheras, alabadas, corridos, alabanzas,* and other types of Mexican popular songs. The Robb Papers contain important material pertaining to the music of Latin America, in particular field notes and song texts transcribed by Robb (a pioneering ethnomusicologist) during trips to Mexico, Brazil, and Central America, interviews with Heitor Villa-Lobos, and other notes, correspondence, and manuscripts dealing with the musical folk traditions of Mexico and the Border region as well as studies of the traditional folk music of New Mexico made in the 1940s by Mexican musicologist and folklorist Vicente Mendoza.

∾ *Manuel Areu Collection of Nineteenth-Century Zarzuelas:* The Library's Manuel Areu Collection documents the history of the *zarzuela* (a Spanish operetta with both music and spoken dialogue) in its Latin American context. Areu and his troupe were instrumental in popularizing the zarzuela across Latin America, especially in Cuba, Mexico, and Guatemala from the last third of the 19th century to the onset of the Mexican Revolution. The collection contains 131 zarzuelas (at least 50 of which are unique), as well as other original music for the theatre and salon, along with playbills and ephemera. The

Areu Collection is consulted and used by zarzuela ensembles from the United States, Spain, and other countries.

≈ *Mexican and Latin American Sheet Music Collection:* A group of some 275 scores, published primarily in the period 1920-1940, containing both lyrics and music of Mexican popular songs. Composers and songwriters represented in the collection include Agustín Lara, Carlos Espinosa de los Monteros, María Grever, Alfonso Esparza Oteo, and Juventino Rosas. This collection is of equal interest to students of popular graphics, as many of the covers were illustrated by prominent Mexican commercial artists. The collection also contains a small number of scores from Cuba, Colombia, Argentina, and Chile.

≈ *Mariachi Spectacular Records:* This collection contains the written records (musical scores, song texts, promotional material, correspondence, and performer biographies) and photographs and videotapes of the Mariachi Spectacular, an annual event established in 1991 by the University of New Mexico in which both traditional and contemporary mariachi are performed.

LITERATURE

Of special note among the Library's holdings of Latin American literary materials are its collections of Brazilian small press publications and *literatura de cordel*. The small press collection contains more than 3,500 books, pamphlets, and magazines issued by alternative, underground, and other non-commercial presses throughout Brazil since the 1970s. It encompasses all genres—short stories, *crônicas*, novels, plays, poetry, and ephemera—as well as critical studies, biographies, literary histories, and other secondary works. The collection's comprehensive scope and the rarity of many of its imprints make it a valuable source for examining different dimensions of Brazilian political and cultural life. The collection of *cordel*, or popular poetry pamphlets, contains nearly 5,000 pieces. *Cordel* (the name refers to the cord or string [*cordão*] on which the pamphlets are hung for display in market stalls and street fairs) is generally composed in verse and its pamphlet and booklet covers often bear woodcut illustrations depicting the *cordelistas*' traditional themes of love, betrayal, and the outlaw hero, as well as the genre's newer treatment of political and social issues. The combination of pictorial and textual elements makes cordel interesting to art historians, anthropologists, folklorists, and social critics, as well as students of literature. The Library continues to add selectively to both collections, all of whose items are individually catalogued and thus accessible to researchers worldwide, via the University Libraries' online public catalog—LIBROS.

Other unique and important Latin American literary materials in the Library's collections include:

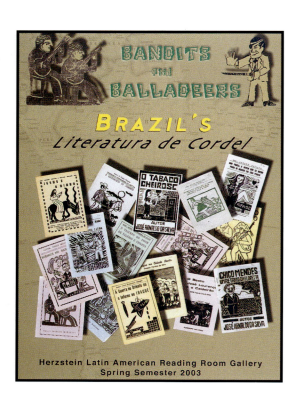

Exhibition poster for display of Brazilian popular poetry pamphlets in the Latin American collection. Tim & Sun Photographic Studio, Albuquerque, NM.

~ **Erna Fergusson Papers:** Journalist and author Erna Fergusson (1888-1964) wrote a number of well-known books on Latin America, such as *Fiesta in Mexico* (1934), Cuba (1946), and *Mexico Revisited* (1955). Her papers include extensive correspondence, records, and research notes relating to her Latin American travels and writings. The material covers a wide spectrum of topics, such as art and the Mexican Revolution, Indian fiestas and ceremonies in Guatemala, problems in inter-American relations, and themes in Latin American literature.

~ **Angel Flores Papers:** Records, correspondence, and other documents dealing with conferences that Flores (1900-1992), a widely-respected critic and translator, organized in the 1970s on such authors as César Vallejo, Octavio Paz, Jorge Luis Borges, and Pablo Neruda. The material includes letters to Flores from many distinguished contemporaries in Europe, the United States, and Latin America, and from writers such as Julio Cortázar, Luis Dávila, and Octavio Paz.

Lithograph by Francis Picabia, one of six done by the artist for the poetical work, *Janela do Caos*, by the Brazilian Maurilo Mendes (Paris: Imprimerie Union, 1949), facing p. 16. Copy 84/197.

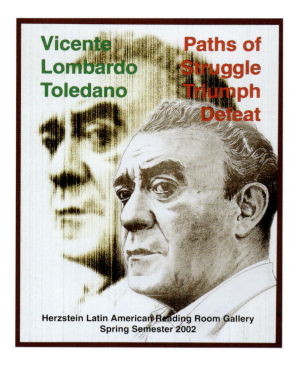

Poster for 2002 exhibition on the life and work of Mexican civic figure and labor leader, Vicente Lombardo Toledano. Tim & Sun Photographic Studio, Albuquerque, New Mexico.

TUNEL Nº1 EN LAS CUMBRES DE MALTRATA.

Lithograph by Santiago Hernández, from Gustavo Baz's *Historia del ferrocarril mexicano . . .* (Mexico: Gallo y Cía., 1874), facing p. 160.

~ *Margaret Randall Papers:* Correspondence, manuscripts, publications, and related material by, from, and about noted photographer, writer, and activist, Margaret Randall (1936-). A large part of Randall's papers documents her active participation in vanguard literary, political, and feminist initiatives undertaken during her residences in Mexico (1960-69), Cuba (1969-80), and Nicaragua (1980-84).

~ *Latin American Crime and Detective Fiction:* A representative group of approximately 250 titles, containing detective thrillers—long a genre of serious writing in Latin America—published between the early 1950s and the 1990s in Mexico, Argentina, Brazil, Cuba, Chile, and Colombia. In addition, the collection includes dissertations and critical studies.

~ *Literary and Cultural Magazines:* The collection holds long or complete runs, in the original edition, of many influential 19th and 20th-century Latin American journals of broad cultural and literary interest, such as *Caras y Caretas* (Buenos Aires), *Nosotros* (Buenos Aires), *Sur* (Buenos Aires), *Revista Chilena* (Santiago), *Anales de la Universidad de Chile* (Santiago) *Revista Nacional* (Montevideo), *Occidente* (Santiago), *Revista da Academia Paulista de Letras* (São Paulo), *Revista Moderna* (Mexico City), and *El Federalista: Edición Literaria de los Domingos* (Mexico City).

ART AND ARCHITECTURE

In no area is the colonial heritage of New Mexico—its creative fusion of indigenous and Spanish styles—better reflected than in the built environment and in the decorative and fine arts. The Library holds a number of manuscript collections that document these expressive forms, the most prominent of which are the *John Gaw Meem Archives of Southwestern Architecture*, the *Bainbridge Bunting Collection of Measured Drawings*, and the personal papers of both Meem and Bunting.

The Meem Archives contain a number of collections that document the architecture of New Mexico and the southwest, but at their core are the drawings, correspondence, perspectives, and other material produced by John Gaw Meem during his long career as an architect and leader in historic preservation. Meem was the master impresario behind the Spanish-Pueblo Revival style, which integrated the indigenous Pueblo and Spanish colonial traditions. His correspondence and related material document his efforts, and those of other architects, artists, and community leaders, to save surviving Spanish mission Churches, *haciendas*, and other colonial edifices and artifacts. Similar material is found in Meem's personal *Papers*. The *Bainbridge Bunting Collection of Measured Drawings* contains architectural plans of more than 200 historic buildings in New Mexico and—like the Meem material—documents unique aspects of the indigenous and Spanish colonial architectural traditions, the modifications made to them in the 19th-century "territorial" style, and their revival in the 20th century. The structures that were drawn— churches, chapels, *moradas*, residences, and other buildings—date from as early as 1606. The personal *Papers* of Bainbridge Bunting (who served in UNM's Department of Art & Art History from 1948 until 1979) contain published and unpublished research materials, notes, reports, drawings, maps, blueprints, and class lectures, pertaining to historic buildings and architecture in New Mexico, the southwest, and Mexico, and to the efforts of individuals, such as Meem, to document and preserve them. The *HABS Measured Drawings of New Mexico Buildings* forms a third source of material documenting the traditional architectural styles of New Mexico. The collection (almost none of which overlaps the Bunting Measured Drawings) consists of 42 duplicate drawings (blue line prints on 432 sheets) from the original collection at the Library of Congress.

In addition to material focusing on New Mexico and the southwest, the Library has several manuscript collections that contain material pertaining to the art and architecture of Latin America in the pre-Columbian and Spanish colonial periods. Of particular note in this regard are the *Frederick A. Peterson Papers*, the *Paul Van de Velde Papers*, and the *Dale I. Perry Papers*.

Espacios íntimos, a hand-made book by Mexican artist Yani Pecanins (Mexico: Cocina Ediciones Mimeográficas, 1985). Copy 1/1.

The Book Arts and The History of Books & Printing

The book arts, or the combination and appreciation of physical and visual elements represented in the production of books or book-like objects, form a particularly rich segment of the Library's Latin American holdings. While this part of the collection is very diverse, several components stand out: artists' books, fine press books, book plates, book covers, and book illustration. These five in turn are enriched by a variety of related material, such as portfolios, periodicals with original artwork, and secondary works of all types printed in limited editions. The range and depth of the Library's holdings in this area create many opportunities for scholars to study both traditional and avant-garde art and art movements in Latin America.

~ **Artists' Books:** The artist's book is a hand-made collaboration among artist, poet or writer, designer, publisher, and printer; with a single person—in some cases—fulfilling all of these roles. Created as unique objects, limited editions, or unlimited multiples, the books take a variety of forms, from accordian folds, to pop-up projections, to hand-sewn codexes, and they often incorporate everyday and organic materials, such as feathers, metal, wood, shells, and glass, or—at the other extreme—beautifully rendered lithographs, serigraphs, and other prints. Their content likewise varies widely, from the overtly political to the purely aesthetic. In recent decades, artists' books have constituted one of the most significant forms of artistic and graphic expression in Latin America. UNM's collection is exem-

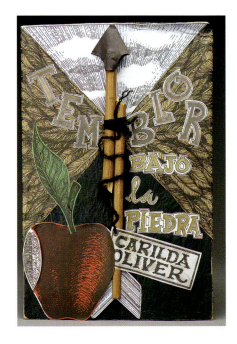

Temblor bajo la piedra, (Matanzas: Ediciones Vigía, 2002). Artist book designed by Rolando Esteva, to honor the 80th birthday of Cuban poet Carilda Oliver Labra. Copy 134/200.

Cover illustration, for Ernesto Reyna, *El amauta Atusparia* (Lima: Ediciones de Amauta," 1930).

plary, containing at present some 250 titles produced over the last thirty-five years by leading figures and graphic workshops: notably: Mirtha Dermisache and Edgardo Antonio Vigo (Argentina), Juan Carlos Romero, Fernando García Delgado, León Ferrari, Teresa Volco and fellow members of the *Grupo Vórtice, Grupo de los Trece,* and other workshops in Argentina, Ricardo Benaím (Venezuela), Anna Bella Geiger, Carlos Clemén, and Silvio Dworecki (Brazil), the *Ediciones Vigía* cooperative in Cuba, Ulises Carrión, Vicente Rojo, Yani Pecanins, Magali Lara, and Felipe Ehrenberg (Mexico), Raúl Quintanilla (Nicaragua), Clemente Padín (Uruguay), Teresa Gazitúa, Claudio Romo, and Guillermo Frommer (Chile), and Patricia Torres and Marcos Paley (Colombia). The collection also includes a substantial number of the books issued by the Bogotá publishing house, *Arte Dos Gráfico.*

≈ **Fine Press Books:** The line separating fine press from artists' books is frequently elusive, but in general, the fine press book is characterized more by its concern for qualities of printing, typography, design, and binding than by the presence of novel artistic elements. Like the artist's book, the fine press book is often published in limited, signed editions. The Latin American collection offers many examples of this genre, two of which bear special mention, the books issued by the Mexico City publishing house, *Ediciones Papeles Privados,* and by the Madrid publisher, *Testimonio Compañía Editorial.* Founded in 1981, *Papeles Privados* has issued more than 40 titles to date. The UNM Library holds the complete collection. Again, as is characteristic of artists' books, the books published by *Ediciones Papeles Privados* often represent a collaboration between poet and artist, juxtaposing word and image in ways that enrich the attributes of each. The books published by *Testimonio Compañía Editorial* are done in a more traditional vein. They comprise limited facsimile editions of classic manuscript books, texts, and documents of the middle ages, the Spanish Renaissance, and the era of Spanish discovery, exploration, and settlement of the New World. The Library holds a substantial number of volumes belonging to the *Tabulae Americae* series.

≈ **Book Plates:** The Library's *Mexican Bookplate Collection* contains nearly 200 individual and institutional bookplates designed and produced between the late 18th and early 20th centuries. Excellent examples of the art of engraving in Mexico, the bookplates belonged to a wide circle of collectors, scholars, and bibliophiles—among them, Joaquín García Icazbalceta, José María Andrade, Nicolas León, Luis González Obregón, and Vicente Riva Palacio. For some plates, several variations exist. The institutional bookplates belonged to convents, monasteries, libraries, booksellers, and bookbinders.

➤ Book Covers and Book Illustrations: A genre not well developed or documented in most Latin American collections, book illustration presents opportunities for examining not just the artwork itself, but a wide range of issues—the search for cultural and national identity, the engagement of artists in social causes, and the use of books by publishers (private and governmental) to promote specific political and economic programs. Geographically, the Library's emphasis is on Mexico, where during the first half of the 20th century book illustration attained particular significance. The collection holds examples of some of the earliest, now-scarce work (etchings, engravings, woodcuts, lithographs, line drawings) done by the masters of book illustration and cover design in Mexico: Diego Rivera, David Alfaro Siquieros, Carlos Alvarado Lang, Angelina Beloff, Leopoldo Méndez, Francisco Díaz de León, Gabriel Fernández Ledesma, Roberto Montenegro, Elvira Gascón, Rufino Tamayo, José Clemente Orozco, Francisco Moreno Capdevila, Fernando Leal, and Miguel Covarrubius. Books, pamphlets, and periodicals illustrated by many of the artists who belonged to or were affiliated with the Mexican print-making cooperative, the *Taller de Gráfica Popular*, are also included, as is the work of more commercially-oriented graphic artists.

In addition to individual titles, the Library holds two distinctive collections in this area: the *Editorial Botas Book Covers Collection* and the *Cuban Book Covers Collection*. The Botas collection comprises 147 books (all first editions) issued between 1919 and the 1950s by Editorial Botas, one of Mexico's preeminent 20th-century publishing houses. Many of the books published by the company were strongly nationalistic and helped disseminate ideas and values promulgated by the government from the 1920s into the 1940s. Their covers were often designed with a similar purpose and serve as vivid examples of the popular graphic art inspired by the aims of the Mexican Revolution. The Cuban collection numbers some 75 proof-state covers, designed and produced between the mid-1980s and the early 1990s, for books issued primarily by Editora Política, the official publishing house of the Communist Party of Cuba. They thus span the last years of Cuba's Soviet-subsidized economy and the initial years of the so-called "Special Period." Stylistically, the covers reflect the eclecticism and experimentation found in the graphic arts in Cuba after 1959, and thematically, they concentrate on portraying the image of the heroic leader and other iconographic symbols of the Revolution.

Bibliographic works and material documenting the history of libraries, book collecting, and publishing in Latin America (with an

Gold-leaf decorated borders, on frontispiece, from Clemente de Jesús Munguía, *Sermón que en la solemnísima* . . . (Mexico: Tipografía de R. Rafael, 1850).

— 29

"The Prado Looking North." Early 20th-century view of one of Havana's principal thoroughfares. [Cuba: Chromolithographs (General File) 998-0011.] Pictorial Collections, Center for Southwest Research/Special Collections, UNM University Libraries.

emphasis on Mexico, Brazil, and southern South America) have been collected systematically by the Library for many years. While the majority of these sources are standard to any large research collection, two groups of material held in the UNM Library merit special attention: books written and published by the Chilean Americanist, José Toribio Medina, and early Latin American sale and auction catalogs:

~ *Medina Imprints:* José Toribio Medina (1852-1930) was the bibliographer par excellence of colonial Latin America. Although his writings spanned more than a dozen fields, Medina concentrated on four interests: biographical and geographical accounts of early Spanish discoverers and explorers, histories of the Inquisition in Spanish America and the Phillipines, histories and inventories of the colonial printing press in Spanish America and the Phillipines, and assembling and editing collections of letters, reports, chronicles, and other material documenting the history of Chile up to independence. Most of Medina's books had been published in editions of one to two hundred copies; several had appeared in editions of fewer than ten copies. The Latin American collection holds more than 130 first editions of Medina's works, including many of the rarest items printed on his own presses, the *Ercilla* (1888-1891), and the *Elzeviriana* (1896-1919).

≈ ***Latin American sale and auction catalogs:*** The latter half of the 19th century saw the dispersal of numerous collections of Latin American manuscripts, books, and other imprints—libraries of rare Mexicana in particular. The greatest collections were auctioned in England and on the Continent, purchased in whole or in part by booksellers, agents, and private collectors. The Library holds the original catalogs for the auction or sale of many of the finest such libraries, notably, those of José María Andrade, José Fernando Ramírez, Charles Et. Brasseur de Bourbourg, Henry Ward Poole, Emperor Maximilian, Eugéne Goupil, J. Court, and portions of the libraries of Lord Kingsborough and Col. Aspinwall. Two of the catalogs were the personal copies of Henry Stevens and contain his marginal bidding notes, showing prices paid by Bernard Quaritch and other booksellers and agents. The collection also holds a number of early 20th-century sale catalogs, such as those issued by W.W. Blake in Mexico City and Karl Hiersemann in Leipzig.

PICTORIAL COLLECTIONS

The pictorial collections, a unit of the Library's Center for Southwest Research/Special Collections, contain photographs, posters, prints, broadsheets, and other visual resources. Extensive Latin American material, some of it unique to UNM, is found in all of these formats. The most significant holdings are the *Sam L. Slick Collection of Latin American & Iberian Posters*, the collection of José Guadalupe Posada prints and related material, the collection of posters, broadsheets, and other publications from the *Taller de Gráfica Popular*, various groupings of 19th century and 20th-century photographs, and portfolios of prints by Guatemalan artist, Carlos Mérida.

≈ ***Sam L. Slick Collection of Latin American & Iberian Posters:*** Formerly known as the International Archive of Latin American Political Posters, the Slick Collection (renamed after the collector who formed it) contains nearly 10,000 images (silk-screen, photo off-set, woodcut, and block print) from Latin America and Spain, the great majority produced between the mid 1960s and the late 1990s. Latin American political posters newly acquired from other sources are also incorporated into the collection. All of the countries of Latin America, as well as Puerto Rico and the United States, are represented in the Slick Collection, permitting the comparative study of such themes as political mobilization and mass communication, opposition to dictatorship and imperialism, the reemergence of democratic regimes, popular movements for literacy, public health, land reform, and human rights, and the adaptation and reworking into Latin American posters of pop art, conceptual art, and other styles

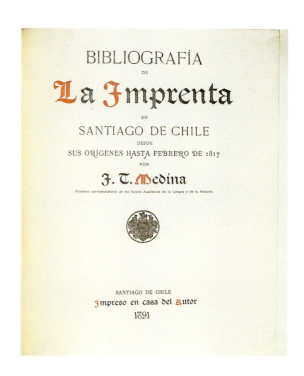

Title page of José Toribio Medina's historical bibliography of the colonial printing press in Santiago, Chile--a work exemplifying Medina's devotion to the art of typography.   Edition limited to 300 copies.

Bibliotheca mexicana . . . (London: Puttick and Simpson, 1880). Catalog of the library of the Mexican bibliophile, José Fernando Ramírez, sold at auction in London in 1880. UNM's copy contains marginal bidding notes, showing prices paid by Bernard Quaritch, Henry Stevens, and other dealers and agents.

uezz.

BIBLIOTHECA MEXICANA
OR A CATALOGUE OF THE
LIBRARY OF RARE BOOKS AND
IMPORTANT MANUSCRIPTS
RELATING TO MEXICO AND OTHER
PARTS OF
SPANISH AMERICA,
FORMED BY THE LATE
SEÑOR DON JOSÉ FERNANDO RAMIREZ
PRESIDENT OF THE LATE EMPEROR MAXIMILIAN'S FIRST MINISTRY,

COMPRISING:

FINE SPECIMENS of the PRESSES of the EARLY MEXICAN TYPOGRAPHERS, JUAN CROMBERGER, JUAN PABLOS, ANTONIO ESPINOSA, PEDRO OCHARTE, PEDRO BALLI, ANTONIO RICARDO, MELCHIOR OCHARTE; a LARGE NUMBER of WORKS, both PRINTED and MS., on the MEXICAN INDIAN LANGUAGES and DIALECTS; the CIVIL and ECCLESIASTICAL HISTORY of MEXICO and its PROVINCES; COLLECTIONS of LAWS and ORDINANCES RELATING to the INDIES. VALUABLE UNPUBLISHED MANUSCRIPTS RELATING to the JESUIT MISSIONS in TEXAS, CALIFORNIA, CHINA, PERU, CHILI, BRASIL, etc.; COLLECTIONS of DOCUMENTS; SERMONS PREACHED IN MEXICO; etc. etc.

DAYS OF SALE :

WEDNESDAY, JULY 7, Lots 1 to 233,   FRIDAY, JULY 9, Lots 469 to 701,
THURSDAY, JULY 8, Lots 234 to 468,   MONDAY, JULY 12, Lots 701 to 934,
TUESDAY, JULY 13, Lots 935 to 1290.

To be Sold by Auction,
BY MESSRS PUTTICK AND SIMPSON,
AUCTIONEERS OF LITERARY PROPERTY AND WORKS OF ART,
AT THEIR GALLERY,
No. 47, LEICESTER SQUARE, LONDON, W.C.,
(Formerly the Mansion of Sir Joshua Reynolds, P.R.A.)

MDCCCLXXX.

and visual languages. In its scope and depth, the Slick Collection is unmatched. The Pictorial Collection houses a number of other Latin American posters, or posters strongly influenced by the popular graphic tradition in Mexico, notably those from its *Holland Collection of World War II Posters* (posters designed by Antonio Arias Bernal, E. McKnight Kauffer, León Helguera, Alexey Brodovitch, Herbert Bayer, et al. for the U.S. Office of War Information and the Coordinator of Inter-American Affairs, and issued or reissued in Spanish and Portuguese-language versions); posters (photo-offsets and silkscreens) done in the 1940s through 1960s by Mexican

389. 1. 6

Stevens 532 MEXICAN. Lecciones Espirituales para las tandas de Ejercicios de 16" —
S. Ignacio, dadas a los Indios en el IDIOMA MEXICANO. Compuestos
por un Sacerdote del Obispado de la Puebla de los Angeles, *calf*
12mo. *Puebla, Imprenta antigua en el Portal de las Flores,* 1841

Quaritch 533 MEXICAN. MANUSCRIT DIT MEXICAIN. No. 2 de la Bibliothèque 3" — "
Imperial. Photographié (sans reduction) par ordre de S. E. M. Duruy,
Ministre de l'Instruction publique, President de la Commission scien-
tifique du Mexique, 1 vol. large fol. *containing 22 photographs*
Paris, 1864
Very scarce and interesting.

ditto 534 MEXICAN. MANUSCRITOS EN MEXICANO. A volume in fol. con- 20" —
taining fourteen original pieces in MS. and three printed ones: the
MSS. occupying two hundred and six leaves. They extend from 1580
to 1847
An INTERESTING and VALUABLE COLLECTION comprising two printed documents,
which we have not seen mentioned by any bibliographer.
The first is—MOTA. Alabado en Mexicano, que contiene los principales Misterios de
nuestra Santa Fe, compuesto por el Br. Dn. Jose de la Mota, Cura . . . . de
Tepecoacuilco . . . . . *reimpresso en Mexico por Zuniga,* 1809. 2 leaves
in 8vo.
The other is a Proclamation in Mexican and Spanish, signed F. S. Tepca, dated
Toluca, Sept. 25, 1847, in which he calls upon the Indians to rise against the
North-American invader: *a single sheet broadside.*

Stevens 535 MEXICAN. METODO FACIL Y BREVE PARA APRENDER EL YDIOMA 1. 6" —
MEXICANO.
ANONYMOUS MS. of the last Century, in 4to. ll. 9.

ditto 536 MEXICAN. Motolinia. The Life and Death of three youths of 1. 13.
Tlascala, who died for the sake of their faith; written by Father
Toribio Motolinia, one of the first twelve missionaries in Mexico,
translated into Mexican by Fr. Juan Bautista 4to.
MS. of 30 leaves. A modern Transcript of the Mexican Original in the National
Museum of Mexico by Don Faustino Galicia Chimalpopoca.

Quaritch 537 MEXICAN. OPUSCULOS VARIOS. MS. collection of various Treatises 14" —
of the 17th and 18th Centuries on literary and historical subjects;
amongst which is a grammatical treatise on the MEXICAN LANGUAGE,
387 *leaves* 4to.

Stevens 538 Mexican. Ordenanzas para provechar los Cofradios allos que han de 6" —
servir en estos Ospitales. En el nombre de la Sanctissima trinidad
. . . aqui comiença una Ordenacion que conpuso y ordeno el
reverendo Padre fray ALONSO de MOLINA, de la Orden de San
Francisco 4to.
ORIGINAL MEXICAN MANUSCRIPT in Gothic letters, 26 leaves. It contains rules for
the administration of the hospitals established by the Franciscans. The author is
the well-known Mexican Scholar, Jo. Alonso de Molina.

ditto 539 MEXICAN. Ordenanzas de su Magestad. A Digest of the early 1. 2"
laws relating to Mexico, MEXICAN MS. 5 ll. *in a small but clear hand-*
writing of the middle of the 16th Century 4to.

Quaritch 540 MEXICAN PAINTINGS. 56.
Two long sheets on which are painted some of the principal events of the Conquest
of Mexico; they date from the 16th Century; copies made at that time from the
originals which existed in the ancient convent of San Francisco in Mexico, and
which have been destroyed long ago. Size 11 ft. 10 in. by 2 ft. 10; and 11 ft. 8 in.
by 23 in.
They contain numerous figures, with explanations in the Mexican language.

ditto 541 MEXICAN. RIPALDA (P. Geronymo de) CATECISMO MEXICANO, que 2. 2.
contiene toda la Doctrina Christiana con todas sus Declaraciones; etc.
dispusolo primaramente en Castellano, y despues para la comun
utilidad de los Indios; y literalmente lo traduxo del Castellano, en el
10

£95. 0. 6

graphic artists, such as Julio Prieto and Francisco Luna, for the
Michoacán-based Latin American adult education agency, the *Centro*
Regional de Alfabetización Funcional en la Zonas Rurales de la América
Latina, known by its original acronym, CREFAL; and a group of more
than 70 posters (woodcuts, linocuts, and off-set litho prints) designed
and printed since the 1970s by the Mexican-American graphic artist,
Carlos Cortéz.

José Guadalupe Posada Material: The Library holds a major archive
of the prints and broadsides done by Mexican popular graphic artist,

FSLN 100. Photo offset [1995?]. Silhouette of the model prepared by Ernesto Cardenal for his sculpture of Nicaragua's revolutionary hero, Augusto Sandino. The poster links the Frente Sandinista de Liberación Nacional to the centenary of Sandino's birth. [drawer 10, folder 16.] Sam L. Slick Collection of Latin American & Iberian Posters, Center for Southwest Research/Special Collections, UNM University Libraries.

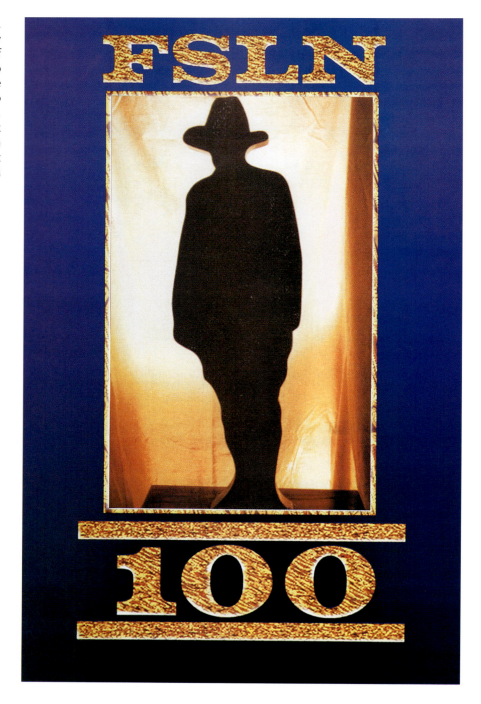

José Guadalupe Posada (1852-1913). The majority of prints (etchings, lithographs, and engravings done between the 1890s and 1913) were part of a collection assembled over a number of years by noted Mexican art historian Fernando Gamboa. The Library's Gamboa collection contains 361 pieces: original broadsides (108), bullfighter portrait series (5), chapbooks and chapbook covers (21), leaflets (19), and restrikes (208). Apart from this collection, the Library holds substantial additional material illustrated by Posada, including chapbooks (ca. 75), children's literature (the complete run, 100 volumes, of the *Biblioteca del niño mexicano* series published in Mexico City in 1900), newspapers (eg., *El Ahuizote, El Hijo del*

By permission of Daniel J. Meléndez Alvira.

José Meléndez Contreras, *Programa de Navidad 1977*. Silkscreen. [drawer 8, folder 1.] Sam L. Slick Collection of Latin American & Iberian Posters, Center for Southwest Research/Special Collections, UNM University Libraries.

Ahuizote, El Diablito Bromista, Juan Panadero), magazines, and penny press publications. There are also additional prints done by this "artist of the Mexican people," housed in two CSWR manuscript collections, the *Mexican Broadsides Collection* and the *Manilla and Posada Prints Collection*. The research value of the Library's Posada materials is enhanced by holdings of secondary works: exhibition catalogs, portfolios of high-quality reproductions accompanied by interpretive material, and important critical studies and appreciations, beginning with the first book devoted to Posada, *Obras de José Guadalupe Posada*, published in 1930 by Mexican Folkways, bearing an introduction by Diego Rivera.

∾ *Taller de Gráfica Popular Collection:* The Library holds a comprehensive archive of work done by the Mexican print-making cooper-

Alexey Brodovitch, *Libres de Miseria . . .* [Freedom from Want]. Photo offset, 1942. [folder 39, item 488.] Holland Collection of World War II Posters, Pictorial Collections, Center for Southwest Research/Special Collections, UNM University Libraries.

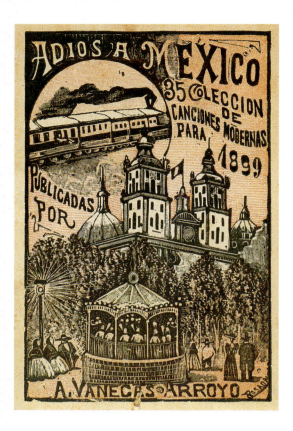

Adios a México . . ., chapbook cover illustrated by José Guadalupe Posada. (Mexico: Antonio Vanegas Arroyo, 1899). [FG0121-FG0130, item 999-019-0114.] Posada Popular Prints Collection, Center for Southwest Research/Special Collections, UNM University Libraries.

ative, the *Taller de Gráfica Popular* (TGP). Established in 1937, the TGP became one of the world's foremost sources of socially-inspired, revolutionary art. The Library's collection, numbering several hundred items, includes posters and broadsheets designed by its founding members, Leopoldo Méndez, Luis Arenal, and Pablo O'Higgins, and by the artists who soon joined or became associated with it: Isidoro Ocampo, Alfredo Zalce, Everardo Ramírez, Mariana Yampolsky, Raúl Anguiano, Ignacio Aguirre, Jesús Escobedo, Elizabeth Catlett, Alberto Beltrán, Angel Bracho, and others. The collection also includes a variety of additional primary source material: flyers, handbills, and related graphic ephemera (cards, calendars, invitations, brochures, exhibition programs); books and serials published by the TGP; a selection of prints made by TGP visiting artists from the early 1940s to the 1960s; original artwork (drawings, sketches, paste-ups, artist proofs); photographic prints of artists who worked at the TGP (including two group portraits of its founding members); and a large number of fine art portfolios issued by both the TGP and its publishing arm, *La Estampa Mexicana*. These holdings are complemented by related material held in the CSWR/Special Collections. Of particular note are books, newspapers (including the *Calaveras* series), and other serials published by the TGP, numerous books and periodicals illustrated by TGP artists, and a collection on 17 microfilm reels of the workshop's organizational records (statutes, minutes, correspondence, contracts, exhibit documentation, and other internal papers) for the period 1937-1960. Among the two or three largest such collections in the U.S., the Library's TGP material offers researchers many items not held in other U.S. repositories.

≈ *Photographs:* The Library has significant holdings of Latin American photography. The images (5,000+, spanning the 1860s to the 1990s in sixty-six collections) are of interest to researchers in many disciplines, including the history of photography. Geographically, the emphasis is on Mexico, with secondary strength in Brazil and Cuba, and selected coverage of other South and Central American countries. Major subjects include archaeology, ethnology, architecture, art, politics, popular culture, landscapes, economic activities, and scenes of everyday life. A variety of photographic formats and processes are represented—*cartes-de-visite*, albumen prints, stereographs, postcards, slides, glass negatives, and modern prints— some of exhibition quality. Of special interest are *cartes-de-visite* portraits of Maximilian and his circle and *tipos populares* (street vendors) by the Cruces y Campa Studio, Mayan monuments taken by Alfred P. Maudslay and Teobert Maler, railroad photographs by William Henry Jackson, *Vistas mexicanas* series by Abel Briquet, political and military leaders of the Mexican Revolution of 1910, and scenes of the Chihuahua campaigns (1910-1913) taken by L.R. Pimentel, Hugo Brehme landscapes of Popocatepetl in eruption, C.B. Waite's tropical

Group Portrait, circa 1943. Photo by Bernard Silberstein. Six members of Mexico's Taller de Gráfica Popular, clockwise from top left: Leopoldo Méndez, Ignacio Aguirre, Raúl Anguiano, Fernando Castro Pacheco, Angel Bracho, Jesús Escobedo. [Mexico: Taller de Gráfica Popular, Artists' Portraits, 998-014-0001.] Pictorial Collections, Center for Southwest Research/Special Collections, UNM University Libraries. Courtesy of Edward B. Silberstein.

plantation views, 19th and 20th-century Mexican mining photographs, Perly Fremont Rockett photographs of Spanish American War scenes, Marc Ferrez's albumen prints of Río de Janeiro, Canudos War photographs, early (1860s) views of Corrientes (Argentina) and environs, 20th-century studies of Andean Indians by George Bunzl, and pre and post-revolution Cuban photographs (including a Ché portrait by Osvaldo Salas). For Mexico, the collection also holds images taken by Guillermo Kahlo, Antonio Garduño, Charles Lummis, José María Lupercio, Enrique Cervantes, Winnfield Scott, Cox & Carmichael, Kilburn Brothers, Mauricio Yáñez, and—from more recent decades—Fritz Henle, Héctor García, Elsa Medina, Eniac Martínez, Pablo Ortiz Monasterio, Antonio Turok, Nacho López, and Mariana Yampolsky. In addition, the collection includes Brazilian photographs of George Leuzinger and A. Frisch as well as photographs taken in various Latin American countries by Roy Rosen.

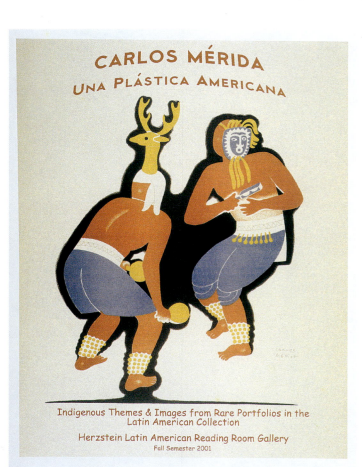

Exhibition poster for display of prints by Guatemalan artist, Carlos Mérida. Tim & Sun Photographic Studio, Albuquerque, New Mexico.

∼ *Carlos Mérida Portfolios:* Between 1927 and 1979, 11 portfolios were published of Mérida lithographs and silkscreens. The editions were all limited, in some cases to fewer than 100 copies, with plates numbered and signed by the artist. The Library holds 6 of these now-scarce portfolios, central to understanding Mérida's synthesis of European modernist techniques and Latin American nativist themes: *Dances of Mexico* (1940?), *Carnival in Mexico* (1941), *Mexican Costumes* (1941), *Estampas del Popol-Vuh* (1943), *Trajes regionales mexicanos* (1945), *Trajes indígenas de Guatemala* (1951).

∼ *19th-Century Mexican Alphabetic Cards:* A set of 24 alphabetic cards, each bearing a lithographic image and popular saying, dating from approximately the mid-1800s. The artist is not identified, but the cards—executed in the satirical style of Hesequio Iriarte and Alejandro Casarín—may constitute a *lotería* game.

HISTORY & THE SOCIAL SCIENCES

The collection of documents that Scholes, Bloom, and Hammond amassed, starting in the late 1920s, focused primarily on the exploits of Spanish *conquistadores* and the development of society and institutions in colonial Mexico. This effort at building documentary collections was continued in subsequent years, but the scope was steadily broadened—chronologically, thematically, geographically. Today, the Latin American collection holds extensive primary source material covering major parts of Spanish colonial America as well as Mexico, Central America, and South America from the Wars of Independence to the present day. The subject matter is likewise rich

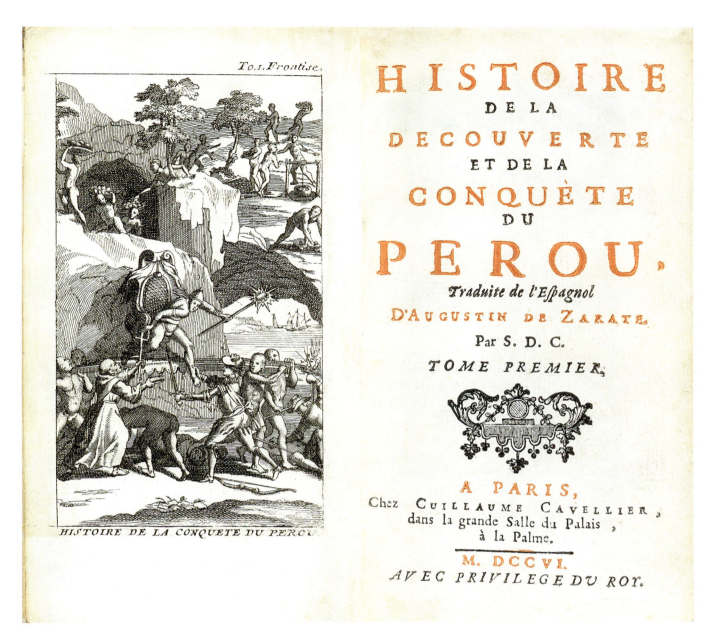

and varied, encompassing economic trends and developments, social
and political movements, religious life and activity, the work of gov-
ernment agencies and departments and hemispheric and interna-
tional organizations, the flow of populations within and across
national and international borders, civil wars and foreign interven-
tions, and campaigns for civil liberties and the rights of women, chil-
dren, and indigenous groups. Collectively, these holdings—micro-
form sets, printed volumes, and original manuscripts and docu-
ments—are listed and described in printed and electronic bibliogra-
phies and finding aids prepared by the Library, or by publishers, dis-
tributors, and individual compilers.

Manuscripts, Archival Collections, and Research Sets

For the colonial period, some of the more significant collections
include: *The Spanish Colonial Research Center Microfilm Collection,*

Nieves Behind the Banana Leaf. Photo of Nieves Orozco, taken in the 1940s by Fritz Henle. [Mexico: Selected Photographers, Box 2: oversize prints: 998-010-0005.] Pictorial Collections, Center for Southwest Research/Special Collections, UNM University Libraries.

Tlachiquero Drawing Pulque. Abel Briquet, 1896. [Mexico: Selected Photographers, General File. Folder: Briquet 2000:001-0001.] Pictorial Collections, Center for Southwest Research/Special Collections, UNM University Libraries.

Depiction of Chimborazo, one of the great peaks of central Ecuador, from Alexander von Humboldt, *Views of Nature . . .* (London: H.G. Bohn, 1850), frontispiece.

(85,000 pages of documents and 4,500+ maps, architectural plans, and sketches from Spanish and Mexican archives, relating to Spanish colonial history in North America), the *AGI/AGN Collection* (bound and unbound photostatic, transcribed, and microfilmed copies of thousands of documents from the Archive of the Indies, Mexico's national archive, and other repositories, dealing with colonial affairs in the Viceroyalty of New Spain), the *Virreinato de Nueva España y Perú durante los siglos XVI y XVII* collection (150+ microfilm reels of correspondence and other documents from Spanish repositories concerning the administration of the two vice-royalties), the complete *cabildo* records for Mexico City, and a major section of the records for Lima, from the founding of the two city councils to the end of Spanish colonial rule, and the *Yale University Collection of Latin American Manuscripts* (microfilmed documents—originals and copies—relating to the civil and religious history of Mexico, Peru, and other parts of Spanish America). Other collections of note for the colonial period include: the *Camino Real Microfilm Collection,* the *Spanish Archives of New Mexico, the Archdiocese of Santa Fe Records, 1692-1850,* the *Bancroft Library MSS Pertaining to New Mexico and New Spain (1581-1904),* the *France Scholes Papers,* the *Colonial Latin American Manuscripts and Transcripts in the Obadiah Rich Collection* (from the New York Public Library), the *Henry A. Monday Collection* (from the Library of Congress) and three sets of microfilmed colonial docu-

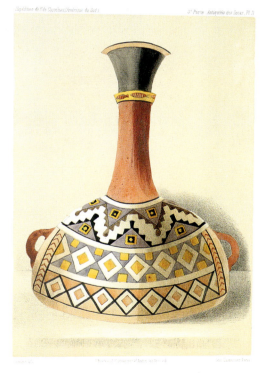

ments recording the history of Texas and northern Mexico under Spanish administration, the *Spanish Archives of Laredo, the Bexar Archives*, and the *Hidalgo del Parral Archives.* The picture of colonial Spanish America afforded by these holdings is rounded out by numerous smaller manuscript and archival collections held by the Library.

The emergence of independent nations and a new political order in 19th-century Spanish America, the opening of the region to new immigrants and to foreign interests, and the growing complexity of state and society in 20th-century Latin America have been reflected in a broadened range of published documentary material. The Library maintains a policy of acquiring these materials on a continuing basis. For Latin America in the modern period, in-depth study is thus possible in and across many areas and fields. Collections of particular note and topical importance include:

≈ *History and Religious Affairs:* The researcher will find major holdings of diplomatic records and correspondence in both print and microform; such as the *British Parliamentary Papers on Central and*

South America, *1800-1899,* the *British Foreign Office Records on Mexico, 1920-1958,* the *British Documents on Foreign Affairs* series, the different series of U.S. State Department records, covering the 19th and 20th centuries, for all of the Latin American countries, and the correspondence and notes sent to the State Department by diplomatic legations posted to the United States from the respective Latin American nations.

The history of the Catholic Church and of Church-state conflict in Latin America, as well as the history of missionary work by other churches and religious institutions in the region, are documented in such holdings as the *CIDOC Collection: The History of Religiosity in Latin America,* the *Board of Foreign Missions: Correspondence and Reports,* for Brazil and Mexico, of the American Presbyterian Church, and the *Serie Conflicto Religioso* (microfilmed manuscripts and imprints, documenting civil-ecclesiastical conflict in Mexico between 1900 and 1945, from the Miguel Palomar y Vizcara Collection in Mexico's National Archive).

The history of socio-economic conditions, of labor, populist, and radical political groups, and of political life in general within specific Latin American states is documented in various collections, such as the *Latin American Pamphlets from the Yale University Library, the Perón Era Political Pamphlets and Monographs,* the *Robert Jackson Alexander Papers,* the *Sutro Mexican Pamphlet Collection,* the collection of *Latin American Anarchist and Labour Periodicals, 1880-1940,* the *Revolutionary Mexico in Newspapers, 1900-1929* set, and the *U.S. Military Intelligence Reports, 1918-1941* (covering Mexico and Argentina).

✎ *Social and Political Movements:* The social and political dynamics of contemporary Latin America, as reflected in the activities of civic and grass-roots organizations, research institutes, university departments, NGO's, mainstream and opposition political parties, and hemispheric agencies, are documented in many collections. These organizations have produced a continuing stream of material—flyers, brochures, broadsides, posters, newsletters, commission reports, conference proceedings, legal briefs, position papers, and other studies—focused on human rights and social justice, the environment, women and gender, indigenism, racial equality, labor, public health, and related issues. The Library holds a wide range of such material. Collections of special significance include: the *NACLA Archive of Latin Americana* (covers 1960s through 1980s), *Brazil's Popular Groups* (1960s—1990s), the *Princeton University Libraries Latin American Microfilm Collection* (emphasis on the last twenty-five years), the *Stoner Collection on Cuban Feminism* (1898-1958), *Mexican and Central American Political and Social Ephemera* (1980-1991), *Amnesty International Country Dossiers* (1975-), *Official Records* of the Organization of American States (1961-), and *Uruguayan Serial Bibliocides* (1971-1984). These large collections, which together com-

Opposite: Cover of the inaugural issue (March 1933) of *Ruta,* a magazine published in Jalapa, Mexico, that championed the radical and avant-garde in politics and literature.

prise many hundreds of microfilm reels, are complemented by three other groups of material: de-classified reports, analyses, and strategic studies of Latin American social and geo-political affairs conducted by U.S. government and executive branch agencies, such as the O.S.S., the C.I.A., the N.S.C. and the State Department, and by independent organizations and institutes (such as the Rand Corporation) contracted to carry out such studies; the Nicaragua and El Salvador components of the documentary collections produced by the National Security Archive; and three manuscript collections held in the Library dealing with civil war, political repression, and human rights in contemporary Latin America: the *Marcos Pérez Jiménez Extradition Proceedings, 1950-1958*, the *Studer Guatemalan Human Rights Collection*, and the *Central America Political Ephemera Collection*.

∼ **Economic Data:** The Library's collection of Latin American historical and political documents is buttressed by holdings of important economic, census, and statistical information from and on the region. Today, much of this material exists in electronic form. Key print and microform sources of economic and statistical material found in the Latin American collection include: *Economic Surveys, 1920-1961: Latin America and the Caribbean* (compiled by the Board of Trade of Great Britain), national and regional development plans prepared by the Latin American governments, population, housing, and other census data issued by national statistical agencies, statistical abstracts, bulletins, and annuals compiled and published by national and international banks, agencies, and commissions, and the complete collection of *Country Reports* for all of Latin America (published by the Economist Intelligence Unit and known between 1952 and the mid-1980s as *Quarterly Economic Review*).

∼ **Major Collections of Interdisciplinary Interest:** The Library holds several Latin American collections that traverse multiple fields. Of special note in this regard are the *T. Lynn Smith Papers* and associated material, the *Columbian Quincentenary Collection*, the *Paul Van de Velde Papers*, and a large collection of South American military periodicals. The T. Lynn Smith material has two principal components, the correspondence, papers, and manuscripts of T. Lynn Smith, a pioneering sociologist of Latin America whose field work and academic career spanned the middle decades of the 20th century, and a linked collection of pamphlets. Smith's papers are vital to documenting the development of empirical rural sociology in the United States, the role of academics in policy-related fields,

Stone-carved façade of the Church of La Merced, from Manuel Atanasio Fuentes, *Lima: or, Sketches of the Capital of Peru . . .* (Paris: F. Didot, 1866), facing p. 24.

the development of systematic sociology in Latin America (Brazil and Colombia in particular), and the planning and implementation of rural sector projects in Latin America from the 1930s through the 1960s. The pamphlet collection contains more than 5,000 titles published in Brazil, Spanish America, and the U.S. between 1890 and the 1950s, focusing on such topics as land tenure, race relations, fertility, migration, and the structure of rural and peasant societies, with primary emphasis on Brazil, Colombia, and the American South and secondary emphasis on Venezuela, Chile, Peru, Mexico, and the Dominican Republic. The *Columbian Quincentenary Collection* (CQC) serves as a permanent documentary record of the 1992 commemoration and of events, on both scholarly and popular levels, leading to it. The collection, which contains many unique items, includes the archives of *Encounters* and *Encuentros* (two leading quincentennial serial publications), the quincentennial files of the Spain '92 Foundation and the N.E.H. as well as records from other national, private, and civic quincentennial commissions and organizations, the quincentennial papers of John Alexander Williams (Executive Director of the U.S. Quincentenary Jubilee Commission) and other figures prominent in the 1992 observance; complete or partial runs of newsletters, magazines, and journals devoted to the Quincentenary, brochures, fliers, press kits and related ephemera, and a large assemblage—not housed with the manuscript collection proper, but linked to it bibliographically—of posters, videocassettes, and other publications, along with the *Voyages to Freedom* travelling exhibition. The CQC is especially rich in documenting the interlocking dimensions of ethnic, political, and cultural conflict that engulfed the Quincentenary, both in the U.S. and elsewhere. The *Paul Van de Velde Papers* contain both print and manuscript material, focusing on topics in Mexican history and archaeology. Of particular note are pamphlets, fliers, and other polemical literature issued by pro and anti-Catholic elements in 1926-27 (including three rare pro-Cristero periodicals); manuscripts documenting civil and ecclesiastical affairs in colonial and republican Oaxaca, assorted material dealing with controversies surrounding the discovery of the Monte Albán site, and plates from the Colección Chavero illustrating archaeological subjects. The military periodicals collection, sometimes referred to as the "Archivo ARMAS" (for *Archivo de Revistas Militares Americanas y de Seguridad*) currently contains seventy-nine journals published by the armed forces in all of the South American countries, augmented by periodicals issued by national police forces and strategic studies institutes. The chronological coverage varies from country to country, spanning in some cases the entire 20th century and more; in other cases, one or two decades only. Holdings are strongest for Argentina, Brazil, Chile, Bolivia, and Colombia. Principal topics covered include national security, armaments, civil-military relations, civil defense, military recruitment and history, and geopolitical strategy. Many of the journals found in the collection are extremely scarce.

EL SABINO DEL PUEBLO DE STA. MARIA DEL TULE.
Estado de Oaxaca.

Depiction of the Sabino Tree, in the Oaxacan town of Santa María del Tule, from *La Naturaleza: Periódico Científico de la Sociedad Mexicana de Historia Natural, años de 1882-1884* (Mexico), Vol. 6, plate 2.

4

Special Print Material: Books, Serials, & Ephemera

—— The Library's collection of books, serials and other printed material from and about Latin America possesses a hierarchy of geographic strengths. Although broad coverage is given to all countries, a stronger emphasis has traditionally been placed on Mexico, Brazil, Argentina, and Chile. And within this emphasis, a particular focus has been given to developing holdings of rare and specialized Mexicana. In this area, several groups of material stand out:

Illustrated Magazines, Newspapers, and Other Publications of 19th and 20th-Century Mexico: The Library holds an outstanding collection of scarce, original periodicals, albums, and other imprints that are essential for documenting not only the course of politics, science, industry, and cultural life in Mexico from the early 19th century through the 1940s, but the intertwined development, in the country's graphic arts, of lithography, political caricature, and social satire. In the political-cultural sphere, partial or complete runs are held to such representative titles, for the 19th century, as: *El Tío Nonilla, El Gallo Pitagórico, El Liceo Mexicano, El Recreo de las Familias, Revista Científica y Literaria de Mejico, El Boquiflojo, El Espectador de México, Repertorio de Literatura y Variedades, Semanario de las Señoritas Mejicanas, La Orquesta, La Tarántula, La Ilustración Mexicana, El Católico, La Cruz, El Ahuizote, El Hijo del Ahuizote, México Gráfico, Cómico, El Mundo Cómico, El Renacimiento;* and, for the 20th century: *Multicolor, El Ahuizote, El Hijo del Ahuizote, Revista de Revistas, Acción, El Maestro Rural, Revista Quincenal de Asuntos Sociales e Ideas, Crisol, Ruta, Frente a Frente, Nuestra Ciudad, Futuro, Proletariado, Capacitación, El Golpe,* and *Hoy.* In the realm of science and natural history, the Latin American collection holds virtually every periodical and monograph of the 19th century that commands attention for its lithographic illustrations, including: *Gacetas de Literatura* (1831 reedition), *El Mosaico Mexicano, El Museo Mexicano, Manual de geología,* Francesco Clavigero's *Historia antigua de México* (1853 reedition), Mariano

Hand-tinted lithograph, in the Mexican satirical weekly, *El Tío Nonilla* [segunda época] 2, No. 10 (7 Nov. 1850), facing p. 162.

Opposite: Frontispiece, by Santiago Hernández, to vol. 1 of Emilio del Castillo Negrete's *México en el siglo XIX* . . . 25 vols. (Mexico: Imprenta de las Escalerillas, 1875-).

Veytia's *Historia antigua de México* (1836), *Boletín de la Sociedad Mexicana de Geografía y Estadística*, *Anales del Museo Nacional de México*, *Anales de Fomento*, *Memoria de la Comisión Científica de Pachuca*, *La Naturaleza*, *Anales del Museo Michoacano*, and *La Escuela de Medicina*. Opportunities abound in these sources to study the work of Mexico's greatest printers, artists, and caricaturists.

~ **Old Mexican Calendarios and Almanaques:** These quaint little books provided information, to travelers and local residents alike, about the country's commerce, agriculture, geography, politics, and religious affairs. Volumes from the 19th century are particularly noteworthy, because of the quality of their design and illustrations (woodcut, lithographs, steel engravings). The Library's collection spans the entire century, from the late colonial period through the Porfiriato, and includes long runs from Mexico's principal publishers of *calendarios*: Mariano de Zúñiga y Ontiveros, Mariano Galván Rivera, Ignacio Cumplido, José María Lara, Manuel Murguía, and José María Rivera.

~ **The Donald C. Turpen Collection on the Mexican Revolution of 1910:** The Turpen Collection, a specialized library on the Mexican Revolution and its aftermath, contains more than 5,000 books, serials, and pamphlets—including many rare and scarce publications. The Collection focuses on the period 1910-1940 and is especially rich in personal memoirs and narratives, biographies of prominent military and political leaders, studies of agrarian, constitutional, and juridical reform, government publications, military accounts, histories of the Revolution on the provincial and local levels, and the records and documents of political, labor, and constitutional assemblies.

~ **Oaxacan Research Materials:** The heart of Paul Van de Velde's library was a remarkable collection of more than 1,500 volumes concentrating on the history, geography, arts, archaeology, and ethnography of the Mexican state of Oaxaca. Comprising monographs, pamphlets, magazines, newspapers, government documents, scientific papers, laws and legislation, dissertations and theses, manuscript books, and printed ephemera, the collection is comprehensive in scope—covering all aspects of life and society in Oaxaca. Among its more specialized holdings are rare 18th- and 19th-century religious imprints and 19th-century newspapers and pamphlets, unique manuscript and typescript books written by Oaxacan historians Manuel Martínez Gracida and Cayetano Esteva, scarce grammars, dictionaries, and linguistic studies (including many published in the 17th and 18th centuries) of the several indigenous languages spoken in Oaxaca, and extensive sets of 19th and 20th-century laws, decrees, and governors' reports. This collection of research materials, widely consulted by scholars from both Mexico and the United States, provides a singularly rich and unified portrait of Oaxaca and its physical

MEXICO EN EL SIGLO XIX.

S. HERNANDEZ, LITOG.ª

LIT. DE H. IRIARTE, MEXICO.

E. NEVE, Editor.
MEXICO.

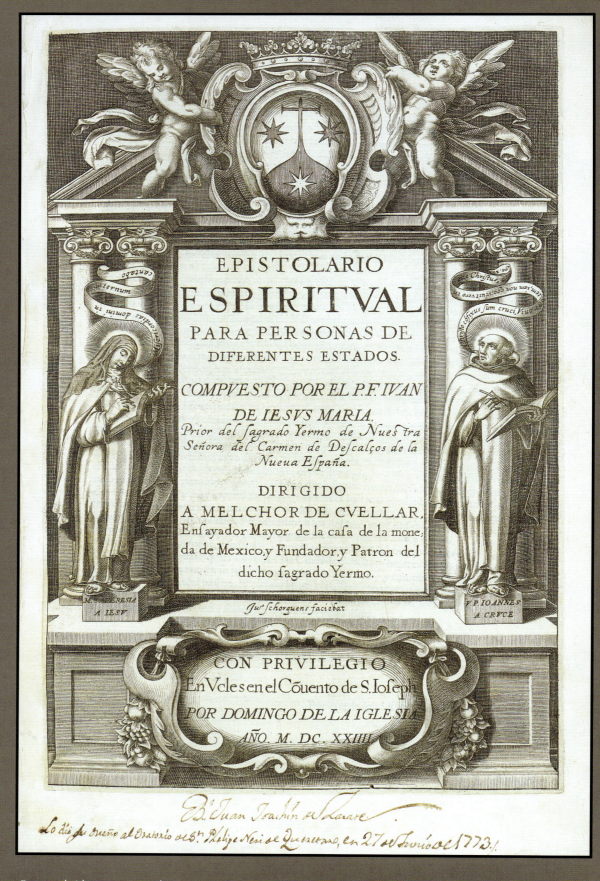

Engraved title page, Juan de Dios María, OCD. *Epistolario espiritual . . .*
(Ucles: En el Convento de S. Joseph por Domingo de la Iglesia, 1624).

Antonio María de Padua, *La Madre de Dios en México* . . . 2 vols. (Mexico:
J. Ballesca: 1890-99?), frontispiece to vol. 1.

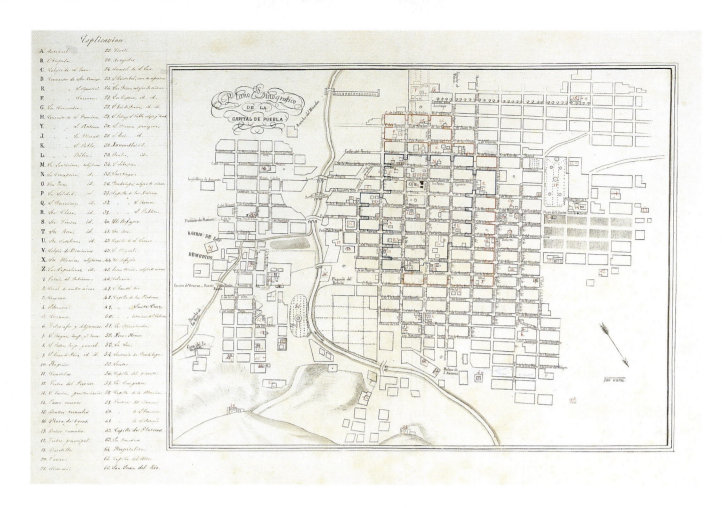

Plano Esdinográfico de la Ciudad de Puebla. Hand-drawn street map of Puebla, Mexico, circa 1850. Map & Geographic Information Center, Centennial Science and Engineering Library, University of New Mexico.

Opposite: Eduardo Vera Cortés, *Programa de Navidad, 1963*. Silkscreen. [drawer 8, folder 7.] Sam L. Slick Collection of Latin American & Iberian Posters, Center for Southwest Research/Special Collections, UNM University Libraries.

and social environment from pre-Columbian times through the early 20th century.

∼ *Mexican Ministerial Reports:* The Library's support for research in 19th-century Mexican history is enhanced by strong holdings of the *memorias* and *informes* issued annually or otherwise by the major government ministries. These official reports are a key source of information concerning foreign relations, religious and military affairs, commerce and trade, the administration of justice, scientific endeavor, and other matters of national interest. In addition to tables and charts, the publications often include illustrations. The Library's holdings encompass all of the ministries and extend (with some volumes missing) from the mid-1820s, when these reports were first compiled, to the end of the century. The ministerial reports are complemented by significant holdings of similar material published throughout the century by many other federal and state government agencies and departments as well as comprehensive sets and individual volumes of Mexican laws, decrees, and legislation.

∼ *Mesoamerican Codices:* The Library houses an extensive collection of facsimile reproductions of Aztec, Mixtec, Mayan and other codices housed in Mexican, European, and North American repositories.

José Rosa Castellanos, *Centenario de la Abolición de la Esclavitud en Puerto Rico*. Silkscreen, 1973. [drawer 8, folder 7.] Sam L. Slick Collection of Latin American & Iberian Posters, Center for Southwest Research/Special Collections, UNM University Libraries.

By permission of José Rosa Castellanos.

These include landmark 19th-century reproductions, such as Lord Kingsborough's multi-volume *Antiquities of Mexico* (1831-1848) and the 1892 folio of codices produced by Mexico's Junta Colombina, the hand-colored, limited edition Librería Antiquaria series published in Mexico City; the Codices Selecti series issued by the Akademische Druck in Graz, Austria, the facsimiles published by the Fondo de Cultura Económica in Mexico, and the hand-made reproductions done in Mexico by Dinorah Lejarazu Rubin. Opportunities for research on the early contact period in Mexico and on the evolving interpretation of its indigenous cultures are further enhanced by the Library's holdings of the original editions of major pioneering ethnographic and archaeological studies done by Mexican, European, and North American scholars and explorers, as well as early drawings of Mayan, Mixtec and other ruins in such works as the *Antiquites mexicaines* of Capt. Dupaix (1834), and the volumes on archaeology, edited by A.P. Maudslay, in the *Biologia centrali-americana* series.

Drawn by Maria Graham.

Engraved by Edw.d Finden.

TRAVELING IN SPANISH AMERICA.

The French Intervention in Mexico: The Library holds a major collection of materials published during the 1860s and after, in Mexico, France, Germany, Austria, and the United States, focusing on the French and European intervention in Mexico (1861-1867). These include political and military histories, biographies, memoirs, ministerial reports, speeches and proclamations, travel accounts, and collections of laws, documents, and diplomatic correspondence, complemented by manuscripts, broadsides, and photographs, as well as newspapers published during the Intervention in both Mexico City and provincial capitals.

Early Grammars and Dictionaries of Mexican Indigenous Languages: A special strength of the Latin American collection lies in its holdings of rare and unusual grammars, dictionaries, and proto-linguistic studies of languages spoken by Mexico's indigenous population. These include some 200 works published between the 1500s and the end of the Porfirian period (1910), treating more than 30 Indian languages, with the strongest concentration on Nahuatl, Mixteco, and Zapoteco.

"Traveling in Spanish America," in Maria Callcott, *Journal of a Residence in Chile* (London: Printed for Longman . . . 1824), frontispiece.

Beginning with the 1571 edition of Alonso de Molina's *Vocabulario en lengua castellano*, the collection includes catechisms and religiously-oriented grammars from the 17th and 18th centuries, a number of unique 18th and 19th-century manuscript books, the complete set of Francisco Belmar's books on the languages of Oaxaca, and numerous works by such early Mexican and European students of ethno-linguistics, indigenous geographic names, and specific indigenous languages as Cecilio Robelo, Nicolás León, Antonio Peñafiel, Francisco Pimentel, Manuel Orozco y Berra, Eduard Seler, and Karl Hermann Berendt.

~ *Baca Family and Bueno Foods' Mexican Cookbook Collection:* The Library holds a large and distinctive collection—books, pamphlets, periodicals, and encyclopedias—on the culinary arts of Mexico from pre-Columbian times to the present. The nearly 800 volumes in the collection (which begins with the country's first known gastronomic imprint, the 3-volume *El cocinero mexicano*, published in Mexico City in 1831), provide comprehensive documentation of Mexico's national and regional cuisine and the social customs and traditions underlying it. The Baca Collection is complemented by more than 600 additional cookbooks and culinary works from throughout Latin America.

~ *Mexican Religious Imprints and Popular Devotional Literature:* Works documenting religious life and practice in Mexico form one of the largest and strongest segments of the Latin American collection. Dating from the first decades of the 17th to the early years of the 20th century, the materials reflect the central role of the Catholic Church in colonial Mexico and the defense of and challenge to this role after Mexico gained independence. The collection is wide-ranging and includes rare Church records and documents (some in bound manuscript form), biographies of saints and missionaries, guides and manuals for parish priests, doctrinal and theological writings, pastoral letters and collections of sermons, histories of religious orders and congregations, ecclesiastical periodicals, works about the cults of the Virgin of Guadalupe and the Virgin Mary, anti-Catholic tracts of the 19th and 20th centuries, and many prayers, hymns, petitions, and other popular devotional literature.

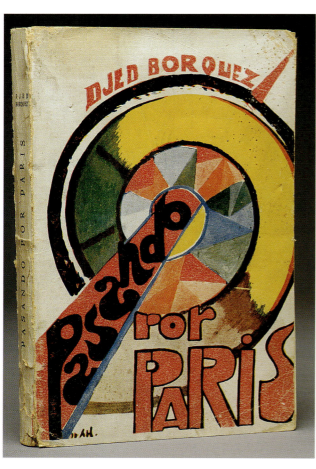

Juan de Dios Bojórquez, *Pasando por Paris (notas de viaje).* (Mexico: Ediciones Lidan, 1929). When Bojórquez published this modest travel account (under his pseudonym, Djed Borquez), he drily observed that its most notable feature was the cover illustration done by the Mexican artist, Dr. Atl (Gerardo Murillo).

~ *Accounts of Travel and Scientific Expeditions to Latin America:* The Library holds an extensive collection of memoirs and accounts written by travelers, merchants, and diplomats who lived in or ventured across different parts of Latin America in the 18th and 19th centuries, by soldiers and free-booters who participated in the Spanish American Wars of Independence and later conflicts and incursions, and by teams of scientists and explorers who were granted licenses,

TROQUILIDEOS DEL VALLE DE MEXICO, AGRUPADOS EN LA IPOMÆA TRIFLORA DE LOS SEÑORES VELASCO.

first by the Spanish Crown and later by the Latin American governments, to carry out investigations (some of which lasted for a decade or more) of the region's land forms, river systems, and unique flora and fauna. The collection covers all of Latin America and is especially rich for Mexico and Brazil.

Hand-colored drawing of tropical birds by José María Velasco, from *La Naturaleza: Periódico Científico de la Socieded Mexicana De Historia Natural, años de 1871, 1872, y 1873* (Mexico), Vol. 2, plate 1.

5

OTHER LATIN AMERICAN RESOURCES IN THE LIBRARY AND UNIVERSITY

—— In addition to the print, microform, and manuscript collections described thus far, research on Latin American topics is supported by other resources and materials, such as maps, films, video cassettes, and compact and video disks, contained in the University Libraries. A website created and maintained by the Library's Division of Iberian & Latin American Resources and Services (DILARES) points the way and provides access to a wealth of information available electronically, from national and international documents to articles and abstracts, bibliographic and reference sources, political and economic reportage, atlases and maps, demographic and statistical data, NGO reports and literature, and images of paintings, photographs, posters, and other visual media. As a multi-departmental unit, the Division integrates traditional public service, collection development, and cataloging operations with specialized research, fundraising, and outreach functions. It organizes exhibitions, speakers' series, and other events; spearheads efforts within the Library to digitize and mount unique collections of Latin American material on the Web, and collaborates with organizations on local, national, and international levels to enhance Latin American and Iberian studies and research resources. The University of New Mexico has played a pivotal role in creating electronic databases with Latin American content, beginning in 1986 with the Latin America Data Base, the first Internet-based news service in English abut Latin America. The Library has been actively involved in a number of these initiatives, such as the *Library Linkages* component of the International Science and Technology Education Consortium (ISTEC), and the *Latin American Social Medicine Database,* pioneered by the Medical School's Department of Family and Community Medicine and the Health Sciences Library and Informatics Center. The Library is also a member of such national and international collection development and document delivery programs as the Latin American Microforms Project (LAMP), associated with the Center for Research Libraries, and the Latin Americanist Research Resources Project (LARRP), part of the Global Resources Program of the Association of Research Libraries. The breadth of its Latin American acquisitions allows the Library to contribute significantly to the international Program for Cooperative Cataloging (PCC) and related Name Authority Cooperative Project (NACO). The DILARES team also assists the Library's Development Office in working with prospective donors and in securing funding for particular projects. The strength of the collections has enabled the Library to obtain more than a dozen major grants from private foundations and the federal government during the last two decades to acquire, preserve, and catalog Latin American materials. A notable milestone for the Latin American collections was reached in 1998 with the opening of the Herzstein Latin American Reading Room, made possible by a gift from Sigmund E. and Barbara Herzstein. Their gift was matched by the UNM Board of Regents, and supplementary support was provided by the El Paso Energy Foundation.

The Library's Latin American holdings are complemented by substantial resources found in many other campus units and repositories. The Bainbridge Bunting Memorial Slide Library (College of Fine Arts) houses 30,000 images documenting Latin American painting, sculpture, architecture, graphics, and decorative arts—Pre-Columbian, Spanish colonial, modern, and contemporary. The University Art Museum has an important collection of Latin American photography, including works by Marc Ferrez, Martín Chambi, Agustín Victor Casasola, Manuel Alvarez Bravo, Graciela Iturbide, Edward Weston, and Tina Modotti. The Art Museum also holds work by Diego Rivera, David Alfaro Siquieros, and José Clemente Orozco, as well as contemporary Latin America prints from the Tamarind Institute, an extensive collection of graphic work produced by artists from Mexico's *Taller de Gráfica Popular*, the Mary Lester Field and Neill B. Field Collection of Mexican Silver, and a collection of tin *retablos*. The Spanish Colonial Research Center, whose core resources are cited on pp. 39 and 42, was established in 1986 by the National Park Service as a joint research project with the University of New Mexico. In cooperation with research entities in Spain, Portugal, and Mexico, the SCRC has developed a computerized documentary collection relating to the history and study of Spanish Colonial Heritage Sites. Additional Latin American resources are contained in the Anthropology Department's Clark Field Archive and Library, the Maxwell Museum Photo Archives, the Law Library, the Health Sciences Library and Informatics Center, and the library of the Latin American & Iberian Institute.

*U*SING THE COLLECTIONS

—— The Library welcomes and encourages the use of its collections by UNM students, faculty, and researchers from outside the campus. Material in the general collection is open to browsing and, with the exception of periodicals published within the last three years (or periodicals held in the Centennial Science and Engineering Library), may be checked out for varying lengths of time by those with borrowing privileges. Access to Latin American research sets in microform is facilitated by a regularly updated electronic guide—searchable by country, subject, and title—maintained on the DILARES website. Manuscripts, rare books, pictorial collections, and other materials that require special handling are kept in closed stacks in the Center for Southwest Research/Special Collections and must be consulted on-site in accordance with the general regulations of the CSWR/Special Collections as well as the specific policies, pertaining to copyright, xeroxing, and the reproduction of images, of the Center's individual units.

For more information about the Latin American collection and related programs and services, please contact the DILARES office, via its website,

<http://elibrary.unm.edu/ibero/>

or call the Program Manager, at (505) 277-0818.

Select List of Publications on the Latin American Collections

Bénaud, Claire-Lise & Oscar E. Delepiani. *Oaxaca: A Critical Bibliography of Rare and Specialized Materials in the University of New Mexico's General Library.* (Occasional Paper No. 5). Albuquerque: Latin American Institute, University of New Mexico, 1992.

Catalog of Luso-Brazilian Material in the University of New Mexico Libraries. Compiled by Theresa Gillett & Helen McIntyre. Metuchen: Scarecrow Press, 1970.

Davidson, Russ. *A Description of Rare and Important Medina Imprints in the University of New Mexico Library.* (Occasional Paper No. 2) Albuquerque: Latin American Institute, University of New Mexico, 1988.

_____. "Las colecciones iberoamericanas en la Universidad de Nuevo México," *Fénix: Revista de la Biblioteca Nacional del Perú* 42 (2000): 106-115.

_____. "La colección oaxaqueña de Paul Van de Velde en la Biblioteca de la Universidad de Nuevo México: Una breve descripción e historia," *Acervos: Boletín de los Archivos y Bibliotecas de Oaxaca* 5, No. 20 (Invierno, 2000): 30-35.

_____. "Analysis of Brazilian Literature Holdings in the UNM University Libraries," *Modernity and Tradition: The New Latin American and Caribbean Literature,* 1956-1994. Ed. Nelly González. Austin: SALALM Secretariat, 1996: 344-353.

_____. "UNM's Quincentenary Archive: Documenting Current History," *Quantum* 7, No. 2 (Fall 1991): 4-7.

"Guide to Latin American Microforms," [DILARES, UNM University Libraries] <http://elibrary.unm.edu/subjects/LAWebGuide/EngMforms/Home.htm>.

"Mexican Popular Prints: José Guadalupe Posada," [Pictorial Collections,

UNM University Libraries] Intro. Stella De Sá Rego
<http://elibrary.unm.edu/posada/>

Mexico in the University of New Mexico Libraries: A Guide to Special Materials and Older Works. Compiled by Russ Davidson & Carol Joiner Albuquerque: University of New Mexico General Library, 1986.

Pedersen, Wendy. "Artifact, Preservation, and Access: UNM's Editorial Botas Book Covers Collection," *Collection Management* 26, No. 2 (2001): 31-41.

Shelflist of the Brazilian Small Press Collection, University of New Mexico General Library. Compiled by Todd Hollister & Russ Davidson Albuquerque: University of New Mexico General Library, 1991.